DOPEamine

Jesse Vacarciuc

AOS Publishing, 2025

ISBN: 978-1-998662-03-6

Cover Design: Meredith Lindsay

Visit AOS Publishing's website:
www.aospublishing.com

Table of Contents

Loving

Change Of POV 2

Le Vent 3

The Wind... 4

11:22... 5

Backseat 6

Lost Sight.. 7

Lighter.. 8

Heresy 9

Voice... 10

There Are Many Ways To Say "I Love You" 11

Fire 12

Russian Roulettes 13

You.. 14

Absorb 15

Eyes 16

Book 17

Home 18

And Yet.. 19

Wish.. 20

I Fall Prey.. 21

Finish Your Work.. 22

Wanting

Spider 24

Canvas... 25

Mercy 26

In Love 27

Oh God... 28

Little Secrets 29

The City 30

Hurting

11:08 32

Mess 33

Break 34

How Long 35

Change 36

Strangers 37

The End 38

Heartbreak 39

Deadly 40

Mistake 41

Bad Habit 42

Alone 43

Name 44

Busy 45

Undress 46

Space 47

A House 48

Plans Of His Own 49

Snow 50

Moving Out Of His Place 51

Going 52

What Love Feels Like 53

Getting Over An Ex 56

Memories 57

Playing 58

Compromise 59

Last Straw 60

To all the boys I've loved 61

Addict 62

Stars 63

Bearable 64

Coming Down 65

Purpose 66

Proud 67

Demons 68

Night-time 69

About To 70

Five Years 71

Trauma 72

Rape 73

Self-Respect 74

Mother 75

Fragile 76

Another 77

Stained Body 78

Metastasizes 79

Mouth Shut 80

Surviving A Fire 81

I Shy Away 82

I Do Not Know Them 84

Broken 86

Once Again 87

Growing

Stop 90

Pieces 91

Beautiful 92

Destiny 93

Strength 94

Waited 95

Porcelain 96

Care 97

Knicks In The Individual That I Am 98

Kindness 99

Vengeful 100

Help 101

Home 103

Survivor 104

Loving

Change Of POV

How do you know you love her?
Do you feel it in the way she bites at her lip
when she thinks?
Do you feel it in the way she sings softly to
herself?
Or maybe is it in her dimpled smile,
Hidden in the creases of her face,
Or maybe is it in her droopy eyes
Whenever she meets you in the morning?
Do you see it in the way
She kisses you like she's afraid she'll never have
that moment ever again?
Do you see it in the way
She looks at you like you are the very reason her
soul glows?
Because I do–
I see why you would love her

-Val

Le Vent

Le vent souffla les feuilles autour de l'arbre
Ton regard me prit au dépourvu
L'air étrangla les poumons de sa douce arôme
Mon amour s'incrusta dans ta peau

Tout bon bon sens s'échappa de mon corps
L'air étrangla les poumons de sa douce arôme
Je me saoulais sur tes "je t'aime" à l'eau de rose
Mon amour s'incrusta dans ta peau

Tu donna aux bourgeons le goût de fleurir
Le vent souffla les feuilles autour de l'arbre
Mes mains dénudèrent ton âme de sa gêne
Ton regard me prit au dépourvu

Mon amour s'incrusta dans ta peau
L'air étrangla les poumons de sa douce arôme
Ton regard me prit au dépourvu
Le vent souffla les feuilles autour de l'arbre

The Wind

The wind blew the leaves around the tree
Your look caught me off-guard
The air strangled our lungs with it's sweet aroma
My love was ingrained in your skin

All good reason escaped my body
The air strangled our lungs with it's sweet aroma
I got drunk on your "I love you" with rose water
My love was ingrained in your skin

You gave flower buds the taste to bloom
The wind blew the leaves around the tree
My hands stripped your soul of its shyness
Your look caught me off-guard

My love was ingrained in your skin
The air strangled our lungs with it's sweet aroma
Your look caught me off-guard
The wind blew the leaves around the tree

11:22

Tell me what you fear, he said

You, I responded

Why? he asked

Because you hold my heart in your hand.
Wrapped fingers around cartilages. Touch etched
into it.
And you alone can break it.

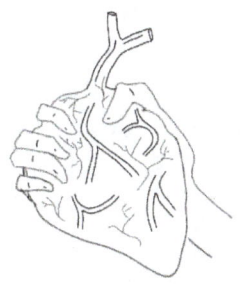

Backseat

Your backseat
Will forever be a sanctuary
To heartbroken souls
That attempt to mend each other
In their clumsy manners
With no desire whatsoever
To abandon their places
As lovers

Kisses and moans
Will fade away
Waiting to be renewed again
And my perfume will stain
Every inch of the seats
While my body will imprint
Its shape in your mind
In your backseat

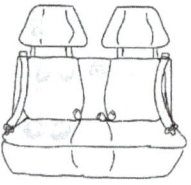

Lost Sight

And I dreamed of your lips last night
And I saw your eyes in my head
And I thought of your hands on me
And I felt your smile

And I think I touched you in my dream
Like an anchor searching for the bottom of the
sea
But the waters were too deep
And the waves carried me away
And I lost my way
And I lost sight of you

Lighter

You revive old flames
Like the flick of a lighter

Tell me, baby
Do you get off on it?

Heresy

I've got your
name on the
tip of my
tongue like
the wine
I've got in
in my system

You're a spell
waiting to
be muttered
in a heretic
attempt to
mend souls
together

Voice

Your voice
Makes me feel
Like I've never
Heard music
Before

I
  Delve
        Into
          The
     Tune
 Your
     Voice
       Makes
    When
 You
   Say
      You
         Love
           Me

There Are Many Ways To Say "I Love You"

"I want you to stay"
"Text me when you get home"
"I wanna be there for you"
"I think you're a genius"
"I like the way you make me feel"
"You calm me down"
"You shouldn't hate yourself"
"Did you have breakfast this morning?"
"I want to help you achieve your goals"
"As long as I have a bed, you have a bed with me"
"I'll be there with you every step of the way"
"You mean so much to me"
"I'll make you feel like God is here"
"I missed you"
"I'll see you tomorrow"
"In that moment, all I could think about was you"
"..."

Fire

Why do we dance
Around the fire
Of our frenzy,
Always illuminated
By the light
Of our passion
But one step too close
And we might
Burst into flames

Russian Roulettes

Hearts fall for
New faces like
Russian roulettes
Loaded and ready
To fire at any moment
And we just gotta hope
This time's the right time

You

Ignite fires
I didn't think
Could burn

You
Pull me in
Closer when I
Least expect it

Tattoo

You
Are spellbound
Into my flesh
Like a

Tattoo

Mark waiting
      To be revived
           Under your touch

Absorb

I don't get to know people
I absorb them–
Absorb the tiny little details
That make them art,
Like the way their lips move
When they say good morning

Eyes

I fall in
      love
          with you
Every time
  I look
      at your
          eyes

Book

I fell in love
With a boy
Who knows
Nothing about
Communication
But guesses what
I'm feeling with
Just a look at
My face

He reads me like a book

Home

You seem like
The home I've been
Looking for

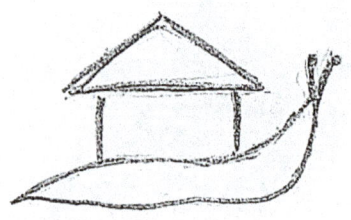

And Yet

It's a storm
It's a crash
It's a firework
It's a symphony
It's anything
And everything
You've ever
Dreamed of
And yet...

Wish

You are, in every sense,
Delightful

I must've thrown enough coins
In a pond

I must've wished on a star
Enough times

To hold you in my arms
At last

I Fall Prey

It's the middle of night,
I fall on the grass
Wet from condensation

I look at you
Smiling at me and suddenly
That spark is renewed
Your stare suddenly
Makes me feel alive
I fall prey
To whatever it is
That you hold

Finish Your Work

Every touch was colour
Every single way you
Put your fingers on me
Painted something new

With this finger was fire
With that finger was the sky
With this hand was a meadow
With that hand was the sea

Your soul was a paintbrush
And I was your paint
And you sprawled me on a canvas
With every intention to
Finish your work

Wanting

Spider

There is something spider-like about the way she
spreads her legs

    She's the black widow buried in the carnations

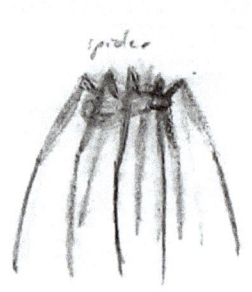

Canvas

He asks me, *Darling, why do you let so many*
men lay their hands on you

I tell him, *Baby, hands are the paintbrushes of the*
mind
I call my body a collaborative piece

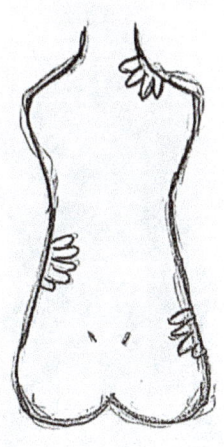

Mercy

Hands wrap around my waist
Like roots tangled in my flesh,
Leaving behind the marks
Of a feeling that can almost
Be expressed with words,
      But not quite

Lips etch their sinful path
Onto my body as it falls prey
To the warmth of your tongue,
Tearing down any trace of
Self-control, and I find myself
      At your mercy

In Love

Would you think I'm crazy
If I told you I was in love
With the things you do to me?

In love with the way you hold
My body in place against yours
Under the swaying trees

In love with your lips
When they kiss their way down
To taste what's inside of me

In love with my hands
When they grasp your shoulders,
Digging their claws in your skin

In love with your voice when
It sings a song of satiety
From the back of your throat

Would you think I'm crazy
If I told you I was in love?

Oh God

I'll make you feel like God is here

I struggle to catch my breath, air hitching the
back of my throat
Oh God you make my knees weak
Show me, please, show me what I've been
missing out on

Little Secrets

My lips on her body
Are a work of art
I knew from her look
She was fucking crazy

The little secrets
I keep with her
Are engraved
In the back of my mind

The City

You gave me
the city
by fucking me
all over it

Hurting

11:08

I told my lover to leave me
Because I wanted him closer
The more I needed him
The more I swore
The more I became desperate
The louder I screamed
And I somehow expected him to get it
I somehow expected him to open me up
And reveal how my bones truly feel

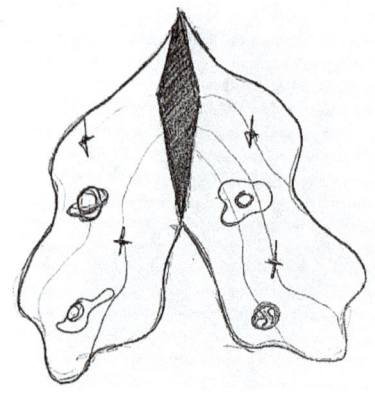

Mess

You're a mess

I know

Pick yourself up

I can't

Why?

Cause you've
got every single
piece of me

Break

I think about the way you could break your fingers, etching them into my skin.

I think about the ways you could break me.

How Long

How long
Till you stop
Loving me
Till my words
Become meaningless
Till my touch
Becomes painful
How long
Till I'm not
The one
Anymore

How long
Till my face
Is pretty no more
Till the butterflies
Fade away
Till your heart
Beats the same
As it did
Before you met
Me

Change

Why can't you change?
I asked him
As he was readying to leave,
Making some stupid excuse
About not being good enough.
Why can't you change?
I asked my reflection in the mirror,
Staring back at the mess,
Thinking I was to blame

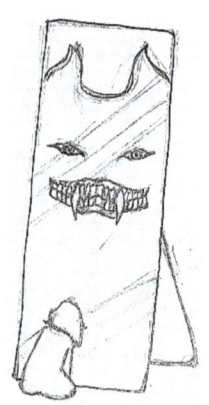

Strangers

We sat like strangers
Waiting for a sign
To act like lovers again

But a sign never came

The End

I feel our story reach an end
I clasp my hands tightly around the measly string
holding us together
I watch it break
I watch you break my heart into pieces
I see you hurl your pain at me,
Going harder with each time I beg you to stop
I know someone will love you just the way you
want,
But that someone isn't me

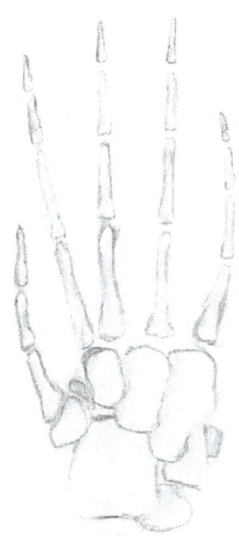

Heartbreak

I think some people are just made to be heartbroken,

At least that's what you've shown me

Deadly

And just when you think you've escaped,
He pulls you back in
And the pain is worse than anything you've ever
felt before
And you wish a broken heart was deadly

But it's not,
So you get back up.

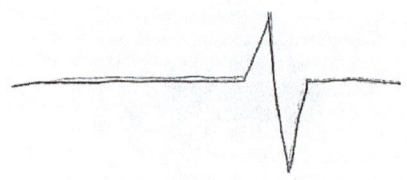

Mistake

There is something so bitter
About the regret in your eyes

Your glare is cold
Your words are empty

Was I a mistake?

Bad Habit

Isn't it just funny?
One man leaves
Another comes
And I don't know whether to call it
An upgrade
Or a bad habit

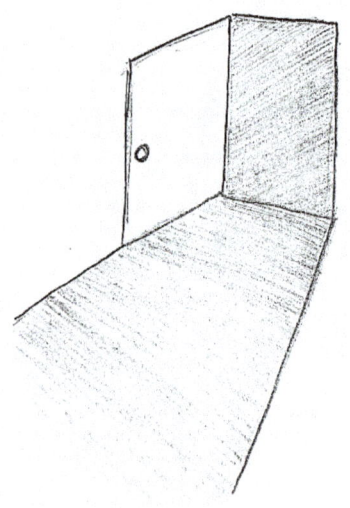

Alone

From one toxic person
To the next
I throw myself around
Like a toy
And there's only me left
To blame
When I'm crying alone
At night

Name

There is disdain in your voice
When you say my name—
You hate not being able to call me
Whatever you want

Busy

Why are you with him
If he only has the time to tell you he's busy

Undress

I undress
And open up
To people
Who can't
Even call
Me
Love

Space

And it hurts more than ever before
Because I truly love him
I love who he is
Inside and out

But he needs space

Lots and lots

Of space

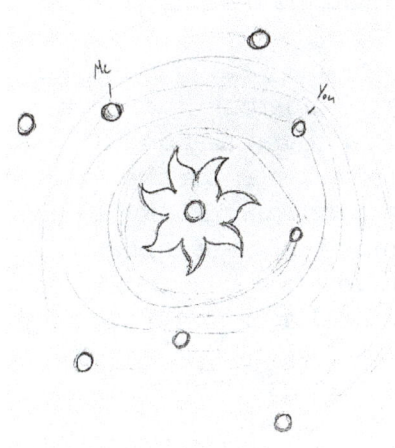

A House

Everything seems to fall out of place
Slowly, the house foundations crumble
The planks crackle and break
The stairs give way under my feet
The roof collapses onto itself
The windows shatter and the drapes,
The drapes that were once so lively,
Are now dull and soiled

Sabotage or careless mistake
From whomever decided to
Build this wretched house
And it   s unstable foundation

I cannot decide but I stand and stare
At the state of something that once
Kept me safe and warm and alive
But now it towers over me like an omen
Preying over everything I failed to give
And everything I failed to replace
But I cannot decide if this stare is his
Or mine reflected back at me on the glass

Sabotage or careless mistake
With no one to quite put the blame on
Because you cannot build a house without
wavering
And you cannot destroy a house without breaking

Plans Of His Own

Disappointment stems from expectation

Kind of like when you expect your bus
To come on time because you're late
For work but the damn bus driver
Has plans of his own it seems

Kind of like when you expect him
To love you just the same as
You love him but he
Has plans of his own it seems

Snow

I met you on a winter night
Smoking away your troubles
Like a burning candle
Melting itself

You were cold like the wind
And I didn't notice
Surrounded by the snow
I was distracted

Snow falling soundlessly
In the middle of the night
Will always fill my heart
With sweet bitter clarity

But it's summer now
And you're still cold
And I wonder where
We went wrong

Moving Out Of
His Place

Oh,
        What a fool I was
To tell myself that leaving
Was going to make me happy

                        It just makes me feel
                        like we're breaking up again

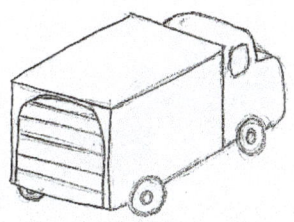

Going

We're always going

                                       going

                                                     going

I'm tired of going

Can we just

                        stay

What Love Feels Like

If someone ever asks me if I know what love feels
like,
I will tell them I know

It feels like giving someone the
Key to the home in your heart
And telling them: here,
You're welcome to come anytime
You'd like

And sometimes they make a
Bit of a mess, but that's okay, because
It's your home and you're
Happy to clean up after
This lovely fellow

But then they forget to lock the
Doors or close the cabinets or
Put down the toilet seat and
You run around trying to
Put everything back in
Place

Seems a bit tiring, doesn't it?

Yes,
Yes it does feel tiring
And my bones ache from
Carrying this boy's messes
While he runs around playing
With his toys

I lose my temper and
Shake the walls with my
Fury,
            and this boy remains,
But his fun does not, nor
Does his interest

He doesn't come back
Home, instead he barges in
Whenever he pleases
And takes whatever he
Wants

Then he doesn't come back

At all,

                              Does it   hurt?

And you leave his toys outside,
If he ever wants to play

                              Does it ache?

And you leave the key
Under the mat

                              Does it burn?

But he doesn't come back
Home

                              Let him go
                    Revoke his right to walk
                        These tiles as if they
                    Were his grounds to lay upon

As if he had built this
Sanctuary with his own
Hands and held the bricks
With his own sweat

He did not build this home
He did not help maintain it
Destroy the key
Change the locks

Getting Over An Ex

In principle
It's pretty easy, no?

Delete his contact
Don't text him

Don't go by his place
Don't look for him

Don't look at the things he liked
Don't think about him

Pretty easy,
Right?

But I still text him on holidays
And send him photos

I still sleep with his teddy
And wear his clothes

And even if I shut him out
And replace him with new lovers

He still looks at my photos
And visits me in my dreams

Memories

All of the memories you gave me
Meant a lot to me,
But all my time you wasted
Meant a lot to me, too

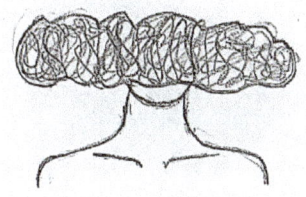

Playing

And just as I
Was starting to get
Over you,

You came right back
Between my tiny
Little hands

Yet somehow
This time is different–

This time your eyes look
Like they're falling for me all over again

But I'm not falling;

This time,
              I'm playing

Compromise

I've always told myself
A relationship is all about

Compromise

And I've been trying to

Compromise

For you when we're not even
In a relationship

Compromise

Just to make you happy

Why can't *you* compromise?

Last Straw

Loving you made me feel
Like I had stepped on the stairs
Of the church at the start of
A sacrament

Loving you was a choice
I made, hoping to see
A future embedded
In our story

Loving you made me want
More from life than any other
Wretched success I could've
Amassed

Loving you made me lose
Myself in the sights of all
The things I could've done
For you

Loving you left me empty,
Unwanting of love and
Anything to do with it
After you

Loving you
Was the last straw

To all the boys I've loved

I will remember
The way you've yelled at me
The way you've stood me up
The way you've laid hands on me
The way you've told me I was unattractive
The way you've told me I wasn't worth it
The way you've told me I wasn't the one you
were looking for
The way you've told me I wouldn't be the last
The way you've looked me in the eyes while
making me cry
The way you've make me feel like a burden

To all the boys I've loved,
I will remember

Addict

I have become an addict–
Everything hurts when I'm lucid;
I just want to stay high
And forget

Stars

as I'm walking down
the midnight streets

high
i

discover that stars
have more stories to tell
when you give them
a soundtrack

Bearable

We desensitize ourselves
To unhealthy things
Just to feel less bad
About ruining ourselves

We lie to ourselves
Just to maintain behaviours
That make our lives bearable
For a few more hours

Coming Down

We as people are divided,
Set aside, separated
Between the ones who are sober
And the ones who are not

Everyone chooses sides
Like a fucking dodgeball game,
Shame is thrown on lack of sobriety
Stories of recovery are muted

So addicts resign to spending time
With other addicts to feel understood,
And habits are reinforced
When there's no one to take example from

Sobriety becomes a distant dream
When you spend your days high

Purpose

I can't keep doing this
I can't keep doing this to myself

I can't keep depending
I can't keep depending on drugs

To make me feel
To make me feel better

I need purpose

- eat before
- drink lots of water.
- get lots of sleep
- no drugs etc

Proud

I've come a far way,
But I'm not proud of who I am;
I can't conquer all my demons
Because getting high is
One Hell
Of an experience

Demons

I have finally met
My *demons*
And I realize that
I never want to feel
Like this
       Ever
          Again

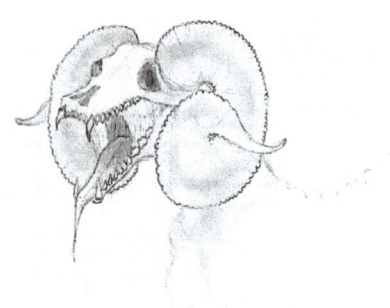

Night-time

It's night-time
And I find myself
Once again
Fantasizing about
The ways
I could take my life
Away

About To

My hands are about to
Let go, my scars are about
To open up, my blood is
About to rise and spill
Like an overflowing river

My goodbyes are about to
Be said, my eyes are about
To empty themselves of
Tears, my body is about to
Give out, my story is about to
End

Five Years

Five years now
I've been calling
The extension number
Of my brain
Leaving endless voicemails
Asking how to get better
How to deal with myself
How to get help
How to get a grip on life
How to fix myself
I cry and I beg
For an answer

Five years now
I haven't got a call back

Trauma

I think the hardest
is coming to terms with what happened to me

To this day I cannot do it

But I have hope that one day-
One day it will only be
memories of a nightmare,
Knicks in the individual that I am

One day I will learn
to define myself as more
than just trauma

One day I will learn
to love being alive

Rape

My eyes foggy,
Devoid of life
Like stained glass
My hands shaky,
Like an earthquake
Inside my mind
My mouth closed,
Yarning to let out
Howls of pain
Every single parcel
Of my body
In and out is on fire
My thoughts wrapped
Around images
Of your sins

Why did you do this to me?

Self-Respect

Self-respect
Is not giving
To the man
Who raped me
The privilege
Of holding
My words
In his hands.

Mother

I have spent
My entire childhood
Learning fear
From you,
So even when
You're not around
I still find myself
Afraid

Fragile

He tells me I'm fragile
With his careful touch
And his worry
But I am not fragile, *baby,*
My body has just been bruised
So many times
That it cannot tell the difference
Between trying to heal
And being broken

And as such it is numb.
Numb to touch. Numb to taste. Numb to feel

Another

As yet again
Another unspeakable thing
Is committed against me
I find the corners
Of the walls
In my apartment
Very soothing

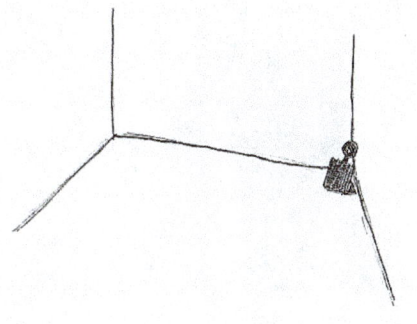

Stained Body

Every hand
Laid on me
Left a mark
And I scrub
And I scrub
But it won't
Come off
And now
I'm stuck
With a stained
Body

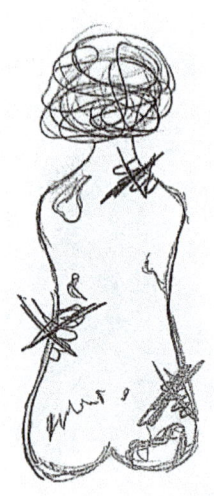

Metastasizes

I think in that moment
I wanted to be the smallest I've ever been
Unfulfilling image in the back of my brain
And in the front of my mirror
This picture wasn't what I wanted to see

This was not my work
Please erase it before it metastasizes

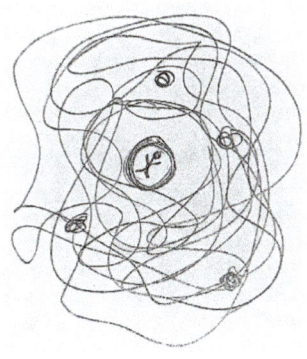

Mouth Shut

I notice that I write least
When I'm at my worst
I think there's just something
About these heavy suicidal desires
That takes away any desire
To create words

Maybe it's the hopeless realization
That no matter how many words I write
To qualify or quantify this misery
It still sits on (breaks) my shoulders
Weighing just as much as it did
When I had my mouth shut.

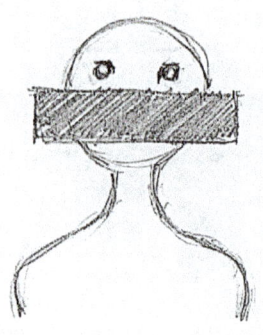

Surviving A Fire

Sometimes... I move in certain ways that for just a second make me feel like I'm waking up amongst the flames once again.

And all I can do is watch everything burn.

And I feel powerless.

I Shy Away

I pride myself in speaking
Of the taboo things that others
Won't talk about
And yet, I shy away from the image
Of your hands laying themselves
On me

Because what you did to me
Isn't pretty
It isn't beautiful
It's not poetic
It's not inspiring

You took my flesh
And you swallowed my tongue
And ground my bones
Into fine dust
Even my nerves felt everything shake

You picked me up like a coin
On the cold concrete
Looked at it, threw it
Into a well, and wished for
Something in return

You must've thought that
Other men violating me
Was an invitation for you
To do the same

So you took me out, then you
Took the sober out of me,
Undressed me in a fucking
Parking lot, and took away my
Privilege to speak

And here I am afraid to speak
Of you, because what if,
Just what if I say your name and
You appear, summoned by the
Weakness in my voice

Because it isn't pretty
It isn't beautiful
It's not poetic
It's not inspiring

It's a pathetic failure to keep
Myself safe in your hands
You, who were once a lover,
Are now a thief of my pride
And my innocence

I pride myself in being a voice
For the taboo little things that
Others run from
And yet, I shy away from your hands
And the shame they left on me
Because I *still* blame myself

I Do Not Know Them

I do not know
This face that sits
And stares into the void

I do not know this person
That you see clinging on
To scraps of a will to live

When the snow will fall
And they will be gone again
This time, they will not return

Sheets will be abandoned
And dishes will be left to rot
Plants will wilt and perish

Water will go stale,
Shelves will collect dust,
Air will grow thick

In the manhole of a rat
Taking refuge in the human vessel
That you see in front of you today

I do not know this person
That cries out to be relieved
Of their humanly duties

They do not strike me
As a character to remark
In the middle of a crowd

I am content with the denial
I am content with not knowing
I am content with acting like this person isn't me

Broken

I am a broken person–
Pieces of me drag themselves
Across the cold concrete
Held together by school glue
And staples

Every day I reapply
The mending materials
Necessary to hold myself together
And every night the glue dries
And the staples rip through my skin

And I do this process
Until my hands bleed
From gluing and mending
And holding together
Every piece that makes me who I am

But sometimes,
I just want to remain broken

Once Again

You've come to haunt me
Once again
I find myself drowning
Once again
I find myself spitting out
All the water
You have pumped
In my lungs
Like a pool of grime
And tears
I've coughed and retched
Every day
Since you have laid
Your hands on me
And I find myself haunted
Once again

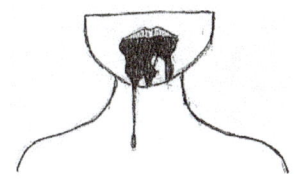

Growing

Stop

Your urgency is staggering

I wish you'd take the time to watch the leaves fall
on a cold, windy autumn afternoon

Pieces

And he asked me,
What has broken you, my love?

Everything,
I said.
Everything around me has chipped a piece off of
who I was,
But I am new now–
The pieces have been changed

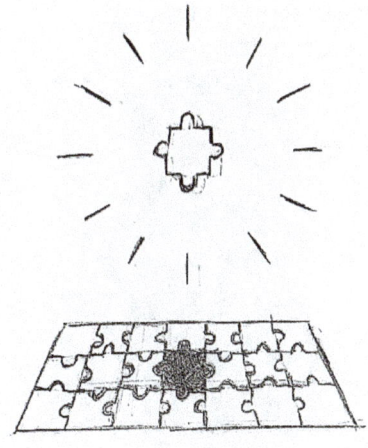

Beautiful

Words dangle from
My fingertips like
Hooks on fishing lines
Above vibrating keypads
Awaiting to show and tell
Tell and tell and tell
Show and show and show
What isn't there but rather
What's inside of me
And who to tell when
Everyone tells on me
So all that's left to do
Is tell my own scars
What they hide
And remind them that
They're beautiful

Destiny

Life has strange ways of telling us it loves us,
Like giving us stars in a dark sky
Or giving us clouds on a bright day,
Hope on a hard night,
Lessons in a peaceful moment,
Reigns holding us back on track
Like strings of destiny

Strength

Don't ever mistake
Her tears
For weakness
Don't ever mistake
Her gentle soul
For vulnerability
She is strength
Embodied
A warrior
Without a sword
She could tear
This whole world
To pieces
And rebuild it
In her image

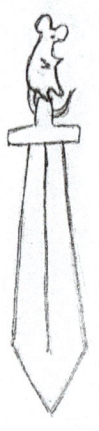

Waited

And I waited-
I waited for my body to die along with my mind,
But it didn't.
    So I gave birth to myself

They do not stop growing

Porcelain

There I was, this vase
Broken in a million pieces,
But amongst the fragments
Past the dust
You found a seed
Willing to grow
So much stronger than
Porcelain

Care

Life is a friend that we do not choose
But rather a friend we have grown with
She may not always be friendly,
But she will always, without fail,
Care about us

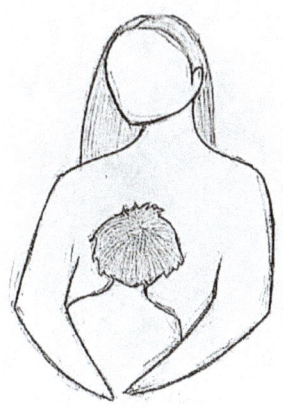

Knicks In The Individual That I Am

So many mean boys
So many hurtful words

Irrelevant
Knicks in the individual that I am

Kindness

There is great strength
In being kind to the people
Who hurt you

You cannot avoid
Being wronged in this life
As I've learned

Therefore you must
Set an example
For all you wish to see

And if kindness is what
You wish to see,

Kindness is what
You need to show

Vengeful

We, as humans, are vengeful creatures. We get others to relate to our pain in the worst ways. People who hurt others are often, themselves, hurting. You aren't to blame for the ways you have been hurt.

When you blame yourself, you become your own aggressor.

Help

Through helping people
I realize one important thing
About helping those who
Need it most,

The suffering
The pain
The hurt
All teaches you to get through it

And when you learn
You teach others
Once you overcome
You help others do the same

But the one thing
That people need most
Other than money
Other than a roof over their head

Is someone to care
Someone to connect to
Someone to show them the bright side
When there seems to be none

I've seen it
I've been through it
And I feel this sadness
Shared by us all

But we cannot all
Be going through
The same thing
Simultaneously

So I only hope
That my long-lived pain
Becomes someone else's
Help

Home

The world
Is my home
The people living in it
Are my family
There will be no exception to this rule

Survivor

I'm a survivor
I've had shit from early childhood
I could either lay down and die or rise above
I chose the latter

- A Familiar

A Note From The Author

Despite all of my experiences, I have never failed to learn a thing or two from them. My lived experience with sexual assault translated into art. I became an independent musician in 2019, with my first single "I Wish" being worked on by me and a producer/friend of mau5trap working at a youth drop-in center. My music career, despite being uneventful, yielded a full album in 2024 titled "Drunk/Sober", containing a collection of 10 songs written by me.

Otherwise, my lived experience got me Google famous in 2020 after doing an interview with CBC talking with them about some of my experiences with homelessness. These experiences also served to build my career in community services, where I started working as a Peer Outreach Worker while in my first year of a Developmental Service Work degree. Since then, I have come a long way. I am a professional artist and musician, a college graduate, a researcher, a program creator, a person with lived experience and an individual who believes they will change the world. I ride the line between being a survivor and being a professional amongst people who have lived the same things as me. I cannot change my past, but I can make the present bearable for people like me. It's not just my story anymore, it's the story of people I work with, people I see in line at the grocery store and people I see waiting for the bus when I drive by a homeless shelter.

Being endlessly driven, I created a program called "The Queer Agenda" in 2022, a 2SLGBTQ+ centered program through the BYFY project in collaboration with CAMH to offer education and support to youth and professionals in the homeless and at-risk sector. Through this work, I've had a chance to present at conferences such as the National Conference On Ending Homelessness and FRAYME.

I have and will continue to use artistic expression to reflect on personal experiences with addiction, homelessness, trauma and mental illness and share the unspoken struggles of youth.

www.ingramcontent.com/pod-product-compliance
Lightning Source LLC
Chambersburg PA
CBHW071204120626
46546CB00006B/2417